W9-BVF-331

The Saving Image

redemption in contemporary preaching

The Saving Image

redemption in contemporary preaching

edited by
john killinger

tidings

1908 Grand Avenue, Nashville, Tennessee
37203

Copyright 1974 by Tidings
1908 Grand Avenue, Nashville, Tennessee 37203
Library of Congress Catalog Number: 73-86375
PRO03B

CONTENTS

INTRODUCTION

In June of 1973 the North American section of the World Council of Churches' committee to restudy the meaning of salvation today met at Rehoboth Beach, Delaware.

One of the truly memorable events of that four-day meeting was a happening designed by Walter Gaudnek, an artist noted for his bold contemporary posters and murals. There is no doubt that the colorful, chaotic happening will be talked about for years by the old boathands and sailors around the yacht basin where it was staged.

Gaudnek had painted huge posters and banners before arriving. Then he rented half a dozen old rowboats. He wanted the participants at the meeting to occupy the boats, row them out into formation on the basin, and raise their paintings aloft.

But other factors entered. First, only one or two of the committee members had had any experience rowing a boat. Second, huge yachts moving in and out of the basin created waves which made the boats difficult to manage. And third, Gaudnek had not reckoned with the wind, which played havoc with attempts to hoist the posters and banners.

This near fiasco of a naval event, however, proved to be an exciting adventure to those involved. Afterwards they laughed and spun tales of how they had almost capsized, how Gaudnek had shouted at them to bring their boats into formation and raise their banners when they were trying desperately to save their lives, and how the natives on the dock and at the boathouse had stared in amusement and disbelief.

From the yacht basin they drove immediately to an abandoned point along the coast where Gaudnek had discovered an old house. The house was bleached by long exposure to the elements, and was falling into ruin. Gaudnek had brought buckets of paint in several colors, and brushes. In the second stage of the happening, participants splashed color onto the old house and the rocks by the sea. A musician played while an interpretive dancer leapt among the stones and driftwood. Two young boys riding by on their bicycles stopped to watch, and were invited to join in the painting. Mounting the roof, they baptized it to the sky in brilliant hues.

Later, back in the sedate environs of the meeting room, the committee watched a record of the happening on video-tape.

A young black pastor from Brooklyn, New York, who was attending his first meeting of this kind, watched the tape and listened to the animated discussion which followed. Finally he could bear it no longer, and drove straight for the cup with an eminently sensible query: ''What does all this have to do with salvation?''

It was a stunning question. Maybe it was already on the underside of everyone's mind. The relationship didn't seem immediately apparent. The committee of churchmen and artists was charged with exploring the meaning of salvation in the contemporary world. What this serious young Christian was asking was the question that nine out of ten members of any church in the country would also ask. How can high jinks such as these have anything to do with human redemption?

Into the moment of silence which followed, there entered the soft, melodic voice of Kathleen Daley, a nun assigned to the Interchurch Center in New York City

"Why, it has everything to do with salvation," she said. "Don't you see? The yacht basin was just a dreary place before we came, like all the other old basins along this part of the coast. The old house was falling down. It was deserted. Everything was dead before we came. Even the rocks were dead. Didn't you see that? They were full of fish skeletons and old crab-shells and pieces of dead wood. Dead. Everything was dead.

"Then we came with the color and the laughter and the music. It all came alive again—the basin, the old house, the rocks, the driftwood. Even the people who watched were caught up in it. They rejoiced as much as we did."

I see this as a parable.

Too much of life is drab and colorless for us today, even in the church.

Salvation has become a matter of doctrine and theology instead of something that defies words in its sudden new way of seeing the world. We have organized it and routinized it so completely that we have made it hard for people to *feel* it any more. We fail to recognize it unless it conforms to our preconceived images of how it occurs and what it looks like when it does.

What salvation is really about is *new life*. It is about color and gaiety and vivacity. It is about the reenlivening of vague and lifeless landscapes, the requickening of dead soulscapes.

Man perceives all things visually. That is, he thinks, plans, and responds to his environment on the basis of images: This is true even if he is physically blind. In that case, he imagines what things are like. And to *imagine* is to conceive an *image*.

The word *image* is also related to *magic*. Magic is the uncommon or extraordinary manipulation of images. It involves the occurrence of something *we could not have imagined*. By the same token, we say that life is magical for us if its images are unusually bright and vivid, if we are seeing it newly minted, with freshness and excitement.

Children readily believe in magic because their world is pulsating with aliveness. The imagery by which they live from day to day is alive and psychedelic. Their universe throbs with possibility.

As we grow older, unfortunately, we cease to see with newness. The images become settled, fixed, routinized. We live as though seeing them, but don't really see them afresh each time. They have become mere symbols of exchange between us and the world.

They enable us to deal with the world without actually seeing it any longer.

This is when the magic goes out of life. We settle into our ruts of acting and reacting, shuttling along through the years with a minimum of response to all the stimuli which are still there, trying to crowd in upon us. We have merely reduced the aperture through which the stimuli can reach us. It grows smaller and smaller.

We watch the children and envy their quickness, their excitement, their intensity of life. We read about primitive people and envy them because they are like children. We miss the magic.

What better definition of salvation is there than to say that it is the return of the magic?

Jesus said it has to do with the blind receiving their sight, and with our becoming like little children again. That is, it is like Gaudnek's revivified landscape: it is concerned with the return of color and possibility where everything seemed dead and foreclosed.

If this is so, it bears important implications for preaching. It means there is a vast difference between preaching and philosophy, or preaching and theology. Philosophy and theology are concerned with ideas and abstractions—with the geometry of thinking. But preaching must have to do with images. It must appeal to the imagination, and help us to see again. The words of the sermon must become pictures, scenes vivid enough for men to enter, so that *a new world happens to them* as the preacher speaks.

This means, in turn, that the preacher is one who constantly lends himself to the creation of new and vibrant images for the task of heralding good news. There is no heralding if the images are not new to the perception of the hearers.

Most preachers want to be true to "the old, old story," and to deliver a reliable account of "the faith once delivered to the saints" in the days of the early church. But ironically, we are *least* true to it when we are most bound to the terms in which it was once given. The words and formulae which once set it forth with power to blaze in men's imaginations become so trite through overuse that they no longer kindle anything for the hearer. This is one reason that preachers with "tired" messages so often resort to hollering and shouting in their sermons: they hope to atone in volume for what they are lacking in genuine vivacity.

The excitement with which the gospel writers called Jesus the "Word" of God had to do with the freshness and newness he brought to their lives. But it is possible for us to make even *that* Word hackneyed and lackluster through mere repetition of how some men said they perceived him.

You see, words all have their origins in events. They are coined to describe what has happened. They are not always brand new, of course; sometimes they are merely reminted—scoured and freshened by the occurrence of new facts or happenings.

To dote on the words themselves, instead of on the events they are trying to narrate, finally wears them thin to the point where they are hardly capable of producing the image of the events. They mistakenly become the objects of attention instead of symbols for the true objects. It is like our seeing a signpost along the road to a certain destination, and accepting the signpost as the destination itself. Or, as a Zen saying has it, it is like fixating our gaze upon a finger pointing to the moon, and never seeing the moon.

It is essential to true preaching, then, that we cease to idolize particular words or images which have been successful in bringing salvation to persons in previous times, and concentrate instead on the discovery of images and idioms which will produce a similar effect in our own time. If Christ is to matter to our generation as more than a cultic symbol—if he is to become a regnant presence transforming the way we look at life—then our ways of witnessing to him must be re-invested with the imagination to galvanize men's thinking about themselves and their environment. Mere orthodoxy for orthodoxy's sake must be set aside as a secondary preoccupation. What we need is the *magic!*

Albert Camus wrote in his notebooks that the man who wishes to be an important philosopher in our day must be a writer of fiction, because it is images that move men, not naked opinion.

He is right, of course. This is what makes novels and movies and television programs so formidable an influence on human behavior in our culture. We cannot behold the world they paint without entering it—and we cannot enter it without being changed by it. It becomes our world because we have entered it. Things are never quite the same again. We are never quite the same.

It was always this way with vital preaching. It "imaged" a new world—called it forth in the minds and hearts of listeners—and thereby altered the environment in which they lived.

We may make jokes about preachers' stories, and define a sermon as "three points and a deathbed tale." But the stories, in the experience of most of us, were the captivating parts of the sermons. They opened the door to a visual world—to a world where we could *see* things, where we could *feel* them, where we could become a part of them.

I remember the grandest evangelistic meeting that was ever held in the church of my youth. The preacher was not a slouch as an intellect, but he was no great mind either. He was a *storyteller*. And what a storyteller! I have never forgotten a detail of a story he told.

One night he preached on the parable of the two sons. The parables are especially pictorial anyway, which is why Jesus used them so much. But this preacher told a story at the conclusion of his sermon that so gripped my imagination that I can never hear the account of the prodigal boy without remembering this tale too.

It too was about a runaway boy who couldn't wait to see the world on his own. And one day he too, broken in spirit like the boy in Jesus' parable, decided to go home. Afraid his old father would not want to see him after his misspent days, he wrote to say he was coming. He would be entering town on the train that ran past the old homestead on its daily run. If the father was willing to see him, he should hang a sheet on the big apple tree near the tracks. The boy would watch for it. If it wasn't there, he would not get off the train at the station, but would just keep going.

As the train neared his home, the boy was seized with panic that the sheet wouldn't be there. Sobbing out his story to the passenger seated by him on the train, he extracted a promise from the stranger to watch for the tree and tell him whether the sheet was there. He himself could not bear to look, and buried his face in his hands.

"Is it there? Is it there?" he anxiously inquired of the stranger.

"Son," replied the man as they roared past the homestead, "that old tree is just **covered** with sheets!"

Later I learned that the story was not original with the preacher from whom I heard it, and my response to it has waned on subsequent hearings. But at the time it was fresh to me, and it struck me with indescribable force. I wasn't merely listening to a tale about a boy wanting to go home; *I was there, I was in that world*. When the preacher said, "God waits like that for you," I went away singing. Life was in technicolor.

I am not making a special brief for this story, but I am appealing for a return to vital imagery in sermons. The obvious power which it has had often draws preachers to old ways of speaking in a bid to recapture it. That is understandable. What we really need, however, is new ways of speaking with power. We need contemporary imagery that is fresh and invigorating, that draws the minds of hearers inward and downward into conspiracy and joy of a world they can *picture* themselves in.

The trouble with old imagery is that it arrests the experience of God and mystery where it is, or, more correctly, where it has been. Persons sensitive to this develop a distaste for the repetitiousness and eventually dismiss religion as a mere magnetic configuration of cliches remaining long after the disappearance of the original magnetic force which called them forth. Persons insensitive to it become religious bores.

We need imagistic and pictorial preaching—but preaching made out of the images and pictures of each new day. Otherwise Christianity becomes the stuff of museums and anthologies, and faith has hardening of the arteries.

The sermons in this slender volume are not the last word on the subject of man's salvation. Their authors did not mean them to be. They are notes on works in progress, as it were—tentative, probing, exploratory. They experiment with new ways of approaching the matter of human redemption. If they sometimes appear to be departures from the faith of our fathers, it is because their imagery and conception is drawn from a world our fathers never saw—a world where computers do the work of years in a matter of minutes and men hurtle through space faster than the speed of sound, where psychoanalysis is probing the depths of the unconscious and communication is instantaneous around the entire surface of the globe. They should not on that account be considered departures. Instead they are extensions. They are the forward edge of faith, and as such are continuous with the past.

Some of the sermons are by-products of a seminar on "The Meaning of Salvation," which I led at Vanderbilt Divinity School in the fall of 1972. It seemed important, on the eve of the massive Key 73 campaign among thousands of participating churches, and in light of the ongoing Celebration of Evangelism, to take a fresh look at the biblical picture of redemption and at the penchant we have in the modern world for developing various substitutes for it. Accordingly, we met each week for fourteen weeks to probe as clinically and imaginatively as we could into the subject.

The substance of my own contributions to the seminar may be found in *The Salvation Tree,* a book published by Harper and Row for use as a study guide in the churches. Some of the sermons in *The Saving Image* are a part of the contribution of other participants in the seminar. In addition, there were film essays, panel discussions, special reports, and multimedia presentations.

Special thanks for this volume are owed to Mr. Harold Bales, associate editor of Tidings, who was a participant in the seminar. It was he who first saw the value of publishing these sermons. Modesty is responsible for the absence of his name from the book's cover. But without him it would never have been a book.

It is his hope and mine that these sermons will provide the stimulus for much new interest in the preaching of salvation.

There is plenty of interest in salvation itself these days—witness the weekly and almost daily articles in public media about the Jesus Movement and other religious concerns. But isn't it important to give creative leadership to this interest, and to provide the framework within which religious revival becomes a constant torch in the dark night of the world instead of a shooting star which flames out almost instantly? We believe so.

Therefore, with thanks to all the contributors and to our colleagues in the seminar whose contributions often underlie what you will see here, we offer this little volume. We think it will brighten your landscape with new images.

John Killinger

Salvation Is Letting the Fish Live to a Ripe Old Age

Mary Richards is a 40-year-old member of First Church downtown. She cannot remember when she was not intimately involved in the life of the congregation. She was baptized as an infant. She grew up in the church school and was confirmed at the appropriate time. She was a leader in the youth fellowship at the church and is now a counselor for the youth. She has three children who have been models of virtue and good behavior. She has never been unfaithful to her husband. She understands what it means to be a Christian and, as far as she knows, has met all the requirements. But now she is 40 years old with a perfect record in religious activity and she has an aching sense of emptiness in her life. Her heart has always been in the right place but somehow she has missed something that she wishes she could identify.

Harold K. Bales is Associate Editor of Tidings, Nashville, Tennessee.

Jim Johnson is a 45-year-old businessman, a Mason, an Elk, a Rotarian and a member of suburban Oak Manor Church. He moved to this church 5 years ago when he bought a home in the new neighborhood. He has been active all his life in the church wherever he resided. He gives a generous portion of his income to benevolent causes. He has never cheated on his income tax. He is a faithful husband. But now he is a puzzled man. His heart is in the right place but there is a peculiar sense of dissatisfaction in his innermost parts. He wonders if he is experiencing something normal for his age. At any rate, something is wrong and Jim doesn't know what it is.

You have no doubt suspected that Mary and Jim are fictitious persons, and you are correct. I suspect, though, that there are countless persons just like them throughout the church. There are persons in every congregation who know all the answers about what it means to be a Christian but whose lives reflect no real joy in discipleship nor any real exhilaration at living out the faith. These are persons whose hearts are in the right place but who have missed a critical clue to purposeful participation in the family of faith. They are persons who have mastered the art of loving in general and missed the point of loving in particular.

It is pointless to love in general. Mary and Jim love God but there is no point in that. Try as they will they cannot translate their affirmation of love for God into anything more than a mechanical mumbling of words. They want to do more than that but God is for them only an idea and a very difficult idea at that. The trouble with loving God is that the whole enterprise is so abstract and impersonal they don't know how to begin.

Mary and Jim love Christianity but there is no point in that. They know that Christianity is a good thing at its best but at its best it is filled with human error and pride. They do care about the portion of Christianity that they participate in, their local churches. But they suspect that most of their fellows share their own sense of unfulfilled hopes and dreams. So there is a nagging feeling of pointlessness about loving Christianity.

Mary and Jim love humanity but there is no point in that. Humanity is an overwhelming generality to whom they cannot speak and to whom they cannot listen. They cannot touch humanity and it is important to touch the object of your love.

One thing is characteristic of the generalized love of Mary and Jim—it is unemotional and detached. It is unthreatening but it is also unrewarding. It is the kind of love that demands constant attention to detail but never demands more than a mechanical response, a routine performance of duty.

The tragedy of many Jims and Marys is that they have not discovered the pointlessness of generalized love. And they have not discovered the power of particularized love. It is pointless to love God in the abstract and Christianity in general. It is a redemptive experience of saving dimension to love Jesus Christ in particular. It is pointless to love humanity but there is saving power in loving a person. In particular, love is redemptive. In general, love is pointless.

I never fully understood the Incarnation or the possibility of truly loving Jesus until I saw a live performance of the rock opera, *Jesus Christ Superstar*. I sat with 8,000 other viewers in an arena where circuses and hockey teams perform on other nights and watched the drama of this man. Incredibly, while others around me were laughing at the comic lines and spirited music, I found myself silently weeping. I could only say with Mary Magdalene, "I don't know how to love him, All I know is he moves me." But suddenly the pointlessness of loving God in the abstract gave way to a deep attachment to this most appealing man, Jesus. I had earlier, through theological reflection, mastered the idea of God but finally I was mastered by a battered and humiliated man.

Do you remember the comment of Jesus: "Love one another"? I have read that phrase many times and have universalized it to mean that I must love everybody in the world—humanity. I think that is an admirable goal but it is certainly a goal that is easily dissipated in a feeling of good will to all persons but actual love for no person. I discovered the context of that phrase recently and it brought new insight to me. Jesus was talking to his disciples. He was saying to them: "If you want other persons to know you are my disciples, you must love each other." He was calling his disciples to particular love, not love in general.

It is pointless to love generally but there is redeeming power in particularized love. A young stock broker was overwhelmed by the pointlessness of the generalized love practiced in the congregation in which he participated. Frustrated, he dropped out of the timid, retiring congregation to particularize his love and practice his faith. He became intimately involved in a rehabilitation program at the state penitentiary. He made friends with a man who had been a prisoner for more than 11 years. Most of the first year and a half had been spent on death row. This young stock broker convinced the young convict that he was a person worth loving and new things began to happen in both their lives. The convict began to have hope and work toward his own rehabilitation. The broker began to have new satisfaction and fulfillment. He began to believe in the possibility of new life in persons.

A letter came to me from the convict a few days after he was granted executive clemency and while he was awaiting his freedom. I think this letter is on the level. He could have used a profession of religious conversion to help gain his freedom but he never made any claim to faith until his freedom was granted. The comments he makes in his letter are his first testimony to faith. Even more, they are an eloquent testimony to the power of particularized love from a Christian stockbroker. The following is part of his answer to a letter I wrote him congratulating him on his new freedom:

> . . . with the little bits here and there that I am fortunate enough to latch onto I have started on the new foundation of a new man. . . . That man being myself. The structure that will someday be me will be a combination of many virtues, many kindnesses, many thoughts and expressions of concern. I can already see most of me as a different person altogether, and I really do think I am going to like me.

I have never been very religious but I do believe. And I honestly love God. I have often wished many times that I could be man enough to be a good Christian. Though so far I have not been able to be this Christian, I am at least another step closer to the sort of man He would have me be. And in my own simple way I love people and want to help anyone I can. I feel this is as close to Christianity as I may ever get.

How many times I have been very near death and it was not allowed to happen. I, as well as some few loved ones and friends, feel there has been a good reason. That there was something for me to do? ? ? I searched for this daily. When I know, I will do it the best I can, and in HIS NAME.

It was pointless for my broker friend to love convicts in general but there was power in loving one in particular. One man is now free. Others remain to be loved particularly.

Arthur Miller's tender little story "Please don't Kill Anything" is about the kind of particularized, sensitive love that reverberates with redemptive power. Sam and his wife were strolling along the beach at sundown when they saw fishermen drawing in their nets. The loaded nets were pulled to the back of a rusty, battered truck where a weather-beaten old fisherman was throwing the good fish into the back of the truck. The inedible and too small fish were being tossed onto the sand where they gasped and flopped about. Sam sensed the tremor of fearful anxiety that ran through his wife as she looked at the fish in the truck. He was relieved as she quickly exclaimed, "They're going to eat them, aren't they?" "They'll feed people," he replied.

Then she looked at the worthless fish littering the beach. She kept pointing to the live fish when they would flop or jerk. "Don't you take those?" she asked the old man. "They're no good, ma'am," was his reply. "Well, don't you put them back?" she asked urgently. "Sure. We put them back," he said and went back to his work.

The lady began to look for something with which to pick up the worthless fish. "You can't throw all those fish back," Sam said gently. "But they're alive!" was her desperate reply. In moments, Sam was picking up the worthless, castoff fish and pitching them into the sea. As they hit the water they would arch and flit quickly into the deep blue.

He was laughing now and she was saying, "I'm sorry. But if they're alive. . . !" The fishermen were watching with smiles on their faces. Finally every one of the fish had been thrown back into the sea and Sam and the tender lady walked hand in hand along the beach. "Some of them might live now till they're old," she said. "And then they'll die," said Sam. "But at least they'll live as long as they can," she laughed.

"That's right," laughed Sam, "they'll live to a ripe old age and grow prosperous and dignified. . . ."

She burst out laughing. "And see their children grown up!" He kissed her. She said, "I love you," with tears in her eyes and they walked home together. *And 50 particular fish swam home.*

One thing is certain about particularized love—it is bathed in tears, echoing with laughter, flooded with emotion. Generalized love is pointless but love in particular is redeeming to the very core of a person. Countless *particular persons* struggle like fish out of water, abandoned on the beaches, lost. The gospel is the proclamation that there is no living thing that is unloved. But that living thing is only truly loved when it is loved particularly. And to be loved particularly is to be given life.

Care and the Uppity Woman

By Ann Denham

This passage describing Jesus' activities is very revealing. Not because it is unique, but because it is so typical. Dip down into any of the Gospels and you will find Jesus wandering around the countryside, touching the sick, making poultices, healing, kissing babies and providing picnic lunches. As a Messiah in a world where such activities are women's work, Jesus is clearly out of step. And although the disciples go along on most occasions, they seem forever baffled by his behavior.

In today's passage they come to Jesus with a practical suggestion: "Let's break for lunch." When Jesus suggests that they are obligated to provide food for the multitude gathered in that lonely place, they don't take this seriously. "Look," they say, "We've only got five loaves and two fishes. Or maybe you had in mind that we go shop for 5000 hungry people!"

Mark contains two accounts of Jesus' feeding large numbers of people. And the second feeding is followed by an interesting scene with the disciples in a boat. The group is heading across the lake on a weekend

Ms. Ann Denham is a United Methodist minister living in Sacramento, California.

retreat and they come to Jesus all in an uproar because they have only one loaf of bread. Jesus, who seems mildly exasperated, says: "You never learn, do you? You've already forgotten! What happened with the five loaves and the 5000? The seven loaves and the 4000? You *still* don't understand!"

And what were they to understand? Not the physical phenomenon of a few buns feeding a vast crowd. If we approach the incident on this level we'll soon be speculating on where they got the 12 baskets to hold the leftovers. No. This event—and all the healing, caring events of Jesus' ministry—points to the power of God at work in the most basic and rudimentary areas of human life. Which is to say that the very God whose power creates all worlds that are is most present and concerned with hungry people at lunchtime.

No wonder they didn't understand! What kind of sense does that make in a world that divorces care from power? After 2000 years it baffles us today. We never see the powerful related to lunch in such a way. The bishop arrives by Cadillac where the women of the church have cooked and arranged a spread. The politician takes a campaign break, while underlings send out for coffee and ham-on-rye. The President speaks and perhaps tours the kitchen where minority workers slice and dice and wait to serve the banquet. In *our* world it is a measure of a man's power that he is *excused* from the basic routines of life.

The consequences of divorcing care from power are all around us. Basic care has become a chore, shunted to those who are powerless to refuse it. To whom fall the jobs of cleaning, feeding, and care? To minorities who can find no other work. To the slow, the uneducated, the inept. And they are poorly paid for their labors. To women, who participate in the status of their husbands within the home, but in the world receive less pay for equal work. To achieve status is to buy out of care. Achieve enough status and you are excused even from the basic task of sustaining yourself. Those in control, removed from the constraints of care, then define our goals in ways which bear little relationship to real life. Persons who never pour their own coffee prescribe for workers, widows, and children.

The separation of care from power is at the heart of all our most pressing problems. What is ecology but a demand for responsible housekeeping? Any housewife can tell you what happens when trash and discards are piled willy-nilly in the basement by persons with more important things to do than sort and bind and drive to the local dump. The basement shrinks, at first imperceptibly. Then debris appears on the stairs, left by those who find storage and disposal too trivial for words. Until one day it backs up in the kitchen, jamming the door, clogging the passageway, delaying dinner.

As those in power have better things to do, the list grows. All systems of care delivery are in trouble: schools, hospitals, institutions, welfare, daycare, retirement, prisons. Our dwindling resources, priorities, even our wars reflect our refusal to imbue care with power.

The uppity Jesus, bringing masculine power to women's work, has shown us the only way out. This out-of-step Messiah, making lunch and washing wounds while speaking with authority, has presented us with the mandate for merging care with power.

More, Jesus has revealed God as caring power. God is a father, the Gospels tell us, and even that translation fails, for father is a formal title, all power and authority. But the Aramaic word that Jesus uses —*abba*—is best translated Daddy. Daddy-god, combining the authority and power of the father and the care and unmerited love of the mother.

The ultimate power of the universe cares and is best revealed in care. That caring is of such dimensions that God moves to take on man's powerlessness. He allows himself to be pushed out of the world, onto a cross. In the words of the song, "he makes our homelessness his home."

We who would follow, who study signs and look for possibilities, are likewise called to be uppity, out of step. To participate in a redistribution of care and power.

Where do we begin—at the bottom and at the top. Tasks of care for those in places of power. Power for those involved in care.

I recently unveiled *my* campaign platform at the dinner table. All persons of power, I said, will be required by law to participate, unassisted, in tasks of basic care. The President, senators, congressmen and the like will all have special arrangements. As a start, Mr. Nixon might be sent to a fatherless family to plan a week's nutritious meals based on 19 cents per person per day. Then off to the local store and home to cook and no fair pulling rank.

All participants in the Pentagon war room, where the games of life and death are played, will go twice a week to daycare centers to wipe noses and pour juice and sweep up crumbs. For those who deploy troops I will demand first hand experience of the long dailyness that goes into producing a human being. There is much evidence that someone in charge believes that persons roll off an assembly line like tanks and guns.

My children say I'm raving. That everyone knows persons of power must be protected from such trivial involvement. Their time is much too valuable.

Very well, let's urge women, whose time traditionally has had no value, to demand, on behalf of care, a piece of the power. It is not happenstance that basic care, so disdained by the powerful, is called "women's work." Women, assisted by minorities, have long been assigned the basic support work of feeding, cleaning, child-rearing and routine care. They make the care-power dichotomy possible. Unlike minorities, women constitute a majority. They remain with the task of care because they consent to do so.

By assuming the whole burden of basic care, women free men for careers in the power structure. The system can then demand the full time and attention of those men for the task and the taskmaster. In exchange a man is offered a chance to buy out of basic care. Often a man's personal life must be handed over to the woman to be managed by proxy. As a fulltime caretaker, whose contribution the structure does not recognize, the woman then becomes dependent upon him for status, financial support and power. And women without male patrons, the divorced, the widowed, the unwed are left powerless. Children without fathers often lack the necessities for growth and health. What may seem like a good private arrangement results in contempt for public care and for caretakers.

Women, I among them, have been willing to remain with the task of care in spite of its negative press. We have often seen through the power game, recognizing food and care as central. But in our failure to demand a piece of the power—to insist on care-sharing for all—because the task is not trivial—we have allowed care to become shunned and powerless. It may be that we must now become uppity, seeking power in the world to support and make central the overlooked necessity of care.

There's an old wives' saying to the effect that we put a woman on a pedestal to avoid looking her in the eye. Some people think that is what goes on on Mother's Day. That those who lead lives uncomplicated by the necessity to render care feel a little guilty and more than a little afraid. Suppose the women of the nation should give notice? So once a year we rush in with testimonials and tokens. Queen for a day. And keep up the good work!

Well, I don't believe that is the only thing at work in Mother's Day. This day—second only to Christmas in phone calls placed and cards and flowers sent—is an attempt to honor, in the person of mothers, body service, unfailing routine, unmerited love. It is all very praise-worthy, but the Christian does not get off so easily.

When power insulates and excuses us from simple, daily care, we are rendered unfit to use that power wisely. The more power we have, the more our decisions are distorted and dehumanized. We approach the absurd as when we destroy a village in order to save it.

When involvement with care leaves us powerless, we are made unfit for caring. Our dependence compromises the nature of our service. Without power to implement care, meeting the simplest human needs becomes a nightmare. As when we say to a woman with no male patron, "You *will* fulfill the obligation of motherhood, despite the fact that we deny you all means to do it."

We as individuals can begin to merge care and power in our own back yards. To develop roles that reflect a new wholeness and not power, decision and independence for some, basic routine and dependence for others.

Why should men be denied the human experience of first-hand care of their children? Not as an occasional helping-out with mother's work, but an equal sharing? Why should women be denied the challenging experience of other work and colleagues, the independence of earning power and decision making? Why should anyone be expected to build a life totally around routine service? Why should anyone be expected in the name of career to fix himself on a narrow aspect of his life, handing over the rest to be managed by proxy? Why should men or women accept definitions which cut off possibilities and which degrade care and dehumanize power?

One family I know of has met this challenge, working out an equal sharing of the tasks of the home and the care of their two small daughters. In addition, both parents are engaged in occupations and share the financial burden of the family. One day after the new system had been in effect some months one of the little girls said to her father, "You know, I used to love Mommy the best, but now I think I love you both the same."

Another couple has reversed the roles, with the wife finding a job while the husband keeps house and works on his dissertation. She admits it was scary to take the responsibility for the support of the family. "And you know," she says, "I have to watch myself or I come home thinking: now why didn't he get the laundry done? After all, I'm out working and he's just home all day."

But you're impatient. I've set you up to save the world and I offer a few trivial examples. I talk about a God who merges care and power and I suggest we take a look at who always does the dishes. Well, it's the nature of our lives that we fail and fall down upon the so-called trivial.

I'm not pushing my own expertise, my chosen life-style. This spring as I have involved myself in meetings and talks and commuting, the burden of care has hung heavy. One day, almost in jest, I said—"You know, what I need is a wife!" What I meant was a person to handle my share of caring. To take over those basic duties which sustain life so that I could get on with more important things nearer the top. Here are my credentials. May I please—for just cause—be excused?

The Christian is never excused. The Christian knows that God is encountered in care and to join that God is to bring to caring, power.

And what of Mother's Day? Putting a woman on a pedestal to avoid looking her in the eye is a heathen holiday. But we can remember and honor those who through selflessness, flattery or force have given themselves that the grace of care might be preserved in the human community. We can ourselves take up the task of care and imbue it with power. And that's the only kind of Mother's Day the Christian can celebrate.

Peanut Butter Hands

By Thomas B. Martin

A Peanuts cartoon, if I remember it rightly, shows Charlie Brown catching a football. Linus says to Lucy, "Charlie Brown has great hands." Lucy cynically replies, "Yes, but they have peanut butter on them."

There have always been individuals and groups who feel it is their responsibility in life to point out the peanut butter on other people's hands. Such activity runs rampant in America today. It is the specialty of the movie magazines, gossip columns, and muckrakers like Jack Anderson. In any election year we see that the major emphasis in campaigning is pointing out the peanut butter on the opposition's hands.

This also seemed to be a specialty of the Pharisees in Jesus' day. The crowds that followed Jesus rejoiced in his great hands—powerful hands of healing to the blind, the lame, the leper; gentle hands extended to little children; open hands washing friends' feet. The Pharisees could only see peanut butter. He eats and drinks with sinners, they cried. He ignores ritual washings. He touches the unclean. He labors with his hands on the Sabbath. Their superficial minds, limited

Thomas B. Martin is pastor of Southminster Presbyterian Church, Nashville, Tennessee.

and limiting, were blinded to all but surface qualities in a man. The Pharisees could not perceive the wonder and greatness of the Soul in their midst. Their vision was limited by law and ritual. They could not comprehend Jesus' message of salvation—that God's love and forgiveness are offered freely to all men—those with clean hands and dirty, saint and sinner, rich and poor, Jew and Greek, the ins and the outs.

The "Good News" left them empty-handed. If salvation is truly free, then the limiting religiosity of law and ritual would no longer sell. Their power, their position, and their advantage was threatened. So they saw to it that those great hands, soiled in loving servanthood, were nailed to a cross. Yet the saving quality of Jesus' hands could not be nailed down. Following his resurrection he appeared to his disciples, authenticated himself by showing his wounds, and commissioned them to carry on the work of his scarred hands.

Talk about peanut butter hands! The disciples were prime examples. These men who shared so intimately in Jesus' life, who had promised so much, who had confessed their undying faith in him, came up short at the time of testing. They fell asleep on guard duty. Peter, the Rock, denied Jesus three times. They all forsook him and ran. Yet, their hands would be extensions of the Master's hands. They would do even greater works than he. Through the "laying on of those peanut butter hands" the disciples would ordain others to carry on the work started in Jesus to men of every place and time.

In light of this let us consider the church in our time. All too often churchmen speak and act as if they were following in the path of the Pharisees rather than in the footsteps of Jesus. Instead of affirming the great possibilities inherent in all men of every race, class, and life style, they dwell on the negative surface aspects of individuals. Instead of preaching the good news of God's free grace and forgiveness that leads to joy and freedom, they preach a restrictive, limited, narrow-minded, pietistic religiosity that for many of us is bad news.

Good news is that all men of every circumstance are fully accepted by Christ and his church. Theologian Paul Tillich, referring to the biblical story of the prostitute who came to Jesus, said that Jesus did not forgive the woman, but declared that she *was* forgiven. The woman came to Jesus *because* she was forgiven—not to be forgiven. She knew he would accept her in love and grace.

The church does not forgive sin, rather it must joyously exclaim that in Christ a person's sins are once and for all forgiven. We in the church, like Jesus, must see beyond the surface. We must not be blinded by human failings, but rather look to find the inner person—the true humanity—the great potential—the soul loved of God.

Because God forgives and loves freely, we in the church can open our doors, our hearts, our hands to any and all men, women and children. In addition, we the "faithful"—can remove our own masks and seek more honest, healing relationships among the brethren.

Is this to say the church is no longer concerned with morals and ethics, with sins and sinnning? Not at all. But it means we need no longer play games such as religious "Schlemiel," which is described by Thomas Harris in his book *I'm OK, You're OK*. In this game the Sinner (who is It) goes through the week foreclosing his tenants, underpaying his employees, belittling his wife, yelling at his children, spreading gossip about his competitors, and then, on Sunday, says a sing-song "I'm sorry" to God and leaves the church with the assumption that "12 o'clock and all's well"— which is the payoff.

The congregation where true acceptance and forgiveness are a reality can move away from a two-faced response to life. What we do becomes more important than what we say.

If we have moral problems, emotional hang-ups, doubts and fears, we can share them with one another. we can support one another, affirm one another. We can forgive because we are forgiven, we can accept because we are accepted.

The church should be a place where men can face the truth about themselves and, supported by love, can change—be converted if you will. In the freedom of the Christian life we can walk together, laugh and cry together, and share a deep encounter with Christ together.

When through loving encounter in the Body of Christ persons are enabled to trust him and believe him, they can change, and something exciting begins to happen in the church. We then have something to shout about, something to celebrate.

Harvey Cox points out, "The earliest gatherings of the followers of Jesus . . . lacked the cultic solemnity of most contemporary worship. They shared a common meal. They had bread and wine, recalled the words of Jesus, read letters from the apostles and other groups of Christians, exchanged ideas, sang, and prayed. Their worship services were rather uproarious affairs . . . more like victory celebrations of a football team than what we usually call worship today."

It is time for Christians to break out of the crusty old molds of repressive religion and learn to experience and celebrate new life in Christ—a life of love, acceptance, joy and sharing. We can do it *where* we are *as* we are. We can share it with all comers. We can rejoice, dance, sing, because God receives all hands into His own:

The peanut butter hands of the school boy,
The strong hands of the athlete,
The skilled hands of the artist,
The gentle hands of the nurse,
The soiled hands of the prostitute,
The fast hands of the con-man,
The calloused hands of the worker,
The soft hands of the idle rich,
The gnarled hands of the old,
The pure hands of a baby,
Your hands,
My hands,
    Amen.

Watching Grace Happen

By Charles Rice

There is that homespun story of the man in a small American town who went down to the tracks every day to watch the train go by. Questioned, he answered: "Well, I just like to see something move that I don't have to push."
We know what he means:
  push-pull
    stop-go,
      buy-sell,
make it, win it, keep it, give it.
Don't just stand there, do something.
  Nothing succeeds like success.
    When you wake up, get up.
God helps those who help themselves.
It's not a bad system, if you can take it.
It's really quite simple.
  Put every person in jeopardy of some sort, and leave no room for failure.
  "Is there no balm in Gilead?"
Replace real human needs with induced desires,
  use the body and all that it enjoys to sell plastics and stuff,
  allow little time for the body's own life,

Charles Rice is Professor of Preaching at Drew Theological Seminary, Madison, New Jersey.

and you have a sure-fire formula for affluence,
   and boredom.
Cultivate appetites that can never be satisfied, unslak-
able thirst for the "good life." Is not life good in itself?
   Change the cars every year, longer, lower, wider,
   smaller;
      raise the hem, pinch the waist,
         button down the collars, unbutton the collars,
           widen the ties, play with the food.
            "God sends food, the devil sends cooks."
Arouse the body, deny the body,
   sell the fold-out, preach the puritan,
      constant sexiness, sporadic sensuality.
      Push-pull, make it, do it, take it.
Show the precious human body in the slicks and on
42nd Street,
   cover it up at home and by the sea.
Nameless, constant, displaced desire.
What do we need?
What do we want?
   "Blessed are the ones who hunger and thirst. . . ."
I want,
   I want,
      I want.
It's not a bad system, if you can take it.
Gross national product rises as steadily as the crime
   rate, our blood pressure.
   10 Billion Sold. Get up and come away.
   "Why do you spend your money for that which is
   not bread,
      and your labor for that which does not satisfy?"

Some people say we Americans aren't as tough as we once were, that we can't take it.

Welfare state: people want everything handed to them nowadays.

What ever happened to the self-made man?

You can't count on anything but taxes, and maybe a heart attack.

Scratch,

push-pull

That self-made man made us all what we are: about a trillion dollars a year.

Get up and go.

Push-pull. Go-stop.

Maybe we can't take it.

We want something to happen to us.

Businessmen ducking into the massage parlors on 8th Avenue and wearing flashy ties and yellow pants on the streets of a booming southern city.

College kids dragging ecstasy out of Mexican weeds.

The housewife learning on a Wednesday morning how to touch people, or reading *The Sensuous Woman*.

Come home, America.

Where is it?

Where can you find a place where you belong just because you were born, just because you are a human being,

that place where, as one of the old-timers said, when you go there they have to take you in?

Funny, but it's usually just when we, as we say, have

arrived, that we start looking out the window and getting itchy feet.

The far country, in our big shag-rug houses.

Status.

Holiday Inns for a week. What would a real inn be like? Sounds funny, holiday *inn*.

Jazzy restaurants. Will you have a cocktail? Steak and lobster cooked together. Surf and turf.

"I am the bread of life."

Grace. Home. About as far as you get from travelcards and managing with Mastercharge.

More like having someone move in on you to make soup and change your sheets when you have the flu.

"He shall never hunger."

Or like getting snowbound.

We had a snowstorm, and I spent a morning at home, away from the office where I manipulate a typewriter and books, and sometimes students. At home, secretly glad, I stood at the window and watched the snow fall,
    everything muffled, changed.

Something happening. You can only stand and watch.

Oh, maybe heat the house,
    fend off nature,
        or even get right out there and start shoveling.

But if you just let yourself go, let it happen,
    let be,

you can feel like a *creature*.

Our bodies live and move and have their life.

Who decides to take another breath or subdivide cells or digest breakfast?

Each day, daily bread: food appears before us

cooked, hauled, picked by people like us that we
don't know;
> warmed by the sun and watered by rain which
> falls on ranchers and migrant workers both.

Every day: people around, some competitors, some
adversaries.

But also parents and spouses and children, friends
and the strangers in the street. The dead.

without them who would have life? Without them who
would want to live?

But do we have life *with* them?

They are all given to us.

Every day something and someone want to happen
to us.

Do you think it will snow?

Now we come to baptize a baby.

Actually, the child has come to us.

Planned parenthood, yes, but a child is always a gift,
like life.

So there is double gift here:
> the child comes to us,
>> "A little child shall lead them."
>>> And we come to baptize the child.
>>>> "For of such is the kingdom of heaven."

This child can't do much for herself now.

Later, she may do many things.

It is as Paul Tillich said:

> "You are accepted. You are accepted, accepted by that
> which is greater than you, and the name of which you do
> not know. Do not ask for the name now; perhaps you will
> find it later. Do not try to do anything now; perhaps later

you will do much. Do not seek for anything; do not perform
anything; do not intend anything. Simply accept the fact
that you are accepted!" *

Wise words,
    wasted on this little child, who doesn't even know
    her own name,
    name given to her before she knows what a name is.
Prevenient grace, we call it, that grace which runs
before us,
    and comes to us,
    like a father glad to see us coming home.
Now of course even children grow up and become
makers and doers,
    even wheelers and dealers and swingers. Push-pull.
    Do it.
Baptism is delayed until pubescence in many
American churches.
There is something in that, when an adult or a teenager
goes down into the water like our Lord,
    his will set to fulfill all righteousness.
And even in churches which baptize infants, there is
that tension which stretches between baptism and
confirmation,
    between the child who can only receive and the
    grown up maker and changer and chooser.
        between creature and creator.
            Creator?
But first it is a gift, that's all.
At the baptismal font, "Well, that *is* a baby."

* **The Shaking of the Foundation** (New York: Charles Scribner's Sons,
1948), 162.

It may be that given the way it is with us in this country
today,
   scrambling and scratching,
     homesick,
       turned in,
         turned inside out,
we need to come down and stand by the baptismal
font and watch grace go by, or come down, or just
happen.
I'll carry the child down the aisle, and show her to you.
Could we get a sense of ourselves being held like that,
in human arms?
   "And at the hour of our death, O Lord."
So, Jennifer Lauren, we come to your baptism, remembering:
   our true status, not in what we can earn, but in the
   good gifts, such as your father and mother would
   give you;
     our place, not in that which we can defend, but
     among the people who hold us up, sometimes
     prop us up;
our home, in God, who calls us his before we know
our own names.

Almighty and everlasting God, heavenly Father, we give
thee humble thanks, that thou has vouchsafed to call us to
the knowledge of thy grace and faith in thee: Increase this
knowledge, and confirm this faith in us evermore. Give thy
Holy Spirit to this child that she may be born again, and
be made an heir of everlasting salvation; through our Lord
Jesus Christ, Who liveth and reigneth with thee and the
same Holy Spirit, now and for ever. Amen.
     (Book of Common Prayer)

Salvation and the First Supper

By Richard L. Sprague

This is a peculiar day to which we have awakened. This day has something very much in common with all of our yesterdays, for this day means that we have come one day further from the kinds of things in our pasts that gave us a sense of belonging and predictability. Today means that we are one day further away from all the memories that have given us strength in the midst of the new. Today means that we are one day further away from all of those events which form the traditions in which we live.

Today means that we are one day further away from the old swimming hole and the first lemonade stand. Today means that we are one day further away from our first report card and our high school graduation. Today means we are one day further away from those good "ole" days in which men were men and everyone worked for what he got and crime was at a minimum, and you seldom heard of wife swapping and murder and lawlessness and general crime in the streets. Today means that we are one day further away from all those family reunions in which the men sat around and talked while the women

Richard Sprague is pastor of Community United Methodist Church in Leavenworth, Washington.

worked in the kitchen. Today means that we are one day further away from the days when our church was filled and everyone got along so well. Today means that we are one day further away from those wonderfully simple times when we churned our own butter and butchered our own meat and raised our own wheat for flour and corn for corn meal. Today means that we are one day further away from our pasts and the richness and meaning and joy that was so much a part of them. That's what today is, and it threatens us. It frightens us. It worries and frustrates us.

But does it challenge us? Does the coming of today challenge us to live in new ways, or does it frighten us into living more in the ways we did before? Does the coming of a new day offer us a new chance at life, or does it remind us of the sweet past in which all of our hopes and dreams and aims reside in a kind of deposit box to which no one has the combination? Is today a word that means we are further away from all that has meaning in our lives? Does tomorrow contain nothing but threats to our comfortable pasts? Is our every meal a last supper symbolizing that we have come hopelessly further from those days in which joy and happiness ruled and simplicity reigned as the order of life?

Are we creatures of our pasts who shrink back from the future in fear and bewilderment? Are we really afraid of the future which begins with each new day? Are we like that cartoon character, the bird that flies backwards so that he can see not where he is going, but where he has been? Are we like the man that

Marshall McLuhan describes who drives into the future with his eyes firmly fixed on the rearview mirror? Are we creatures of history and not made for the future but forced to enter it anyway because that's the way time progresses? Or do we rise with the sense of expectation on our hearts each new day? Do we say with the poet, e. e. cummings,

> I who have died am alive again today,
> and this is the sun's birthday; this is the birth-
> day of life and of love and wings and of the
> gay great happening illimitably earth.

My guess is that many of us find ourselves more and more inclined to cling to the things of our pasts. As we grow older we become more dependent upon the things that are predictable and familiar. We seem to move further away from new life every day because new life is threatening, unpredictable, unfamiliar, and, well, "we've never done it that way before."

I'm wondering if we don't really want to be saved from all the things that frustrate and confuse us, that frighten and hurt us, that unsettle us, that call us into question and demand we make changes? It seems as if we who meet each new day with fear and trembling want to be saved from the bonds of the future; that we who can't cope with the variety of things that are changing in our society and our community want to be saved from them by turning the church into some kind of refuge; a sanctuary away from the world, a "shelter from the stormy blast and our eternal home." We want to be released from the chains of the new.

We want freedom from those things that threaten to dismember our souls and unsettle us, and we say to ourselves: "O God, save us from today which takes us one day further away from our pasts which we love so much." Isn't that what we want to be saved from— the unfamiliar—the new? Save us from tomorrow! Give us back our pasts to live again, all over again, tomorrow and tomorrow and tomorrow.

A few moments ago I asked this question: "Is our every meal a last supper symbolizing that we have come hopelessly further from those days in which joy and happiness ruled and simplicity reigned as the order of life?" In other words, do we see each day as taking us further away from the old swimming hole, the lemonade stand, the raft trip down the river, our first report card, the days of our childhood that we loved so well? Do we see each day as another end of the good life when life moved slowly and easily to the tunes of freedom and happiness? Is every meal a last supper symbolizing this daily progression away from all the things of our pasts that we loved so much? Or do we meet each day with the attitude of that song, "Today is the First Day of the Rest of Your Life"? Are our meals *first* suppers symbolizing growth and change and newness; an unconditional acceptance of tomorrow?

This morning we are celebrating the sacrament of communion, the Last Supper, as are others all around the world. This is a memorial. The celebration is patterned after the last meal Jesus had with his apostolic family in that upper room many years ago. But was that really a last supper? Was that gathering of close friends their way of closing the door on those wonderful moments they had shared together? Was that the end of anything, or was it really the beginning of something that has grown and changed and matured over the centuries? I choose to think that that which we celebrate in symbol this morning was not the last supper, but the first supper of a new covenant; a new agreement in which the peace-makers, the pure in heart, the meek, the humble, those who loved others, were affirmed and celebrated and held up as the ideal. I choose to think of this first supper that we are going to share this morning as a symbol of our willingness to meet tomorrow with our eyes fixed firmly on the road ahead. And isn't that what Jesus of Nazareth was doing? Breaking bread in celebration of the coming ministry of those who would follow him? Jesus was sharing the first supper of the new covenant in which the very elements of life, body and blood, were celebrated, shared, and dedicated.

Well, it's our turn. It's our turn to face the new. It's our turn to share in the first supper of the new covenant. And perhaps at this table a life will be changed. Perhaps we will begin to see past yesterday and the old swimming hole and commit those wonderful memories to the histories in which we dwell, and for just one short moment catch a vision of the rest of our lives that begin at this table today. Perhaps we will slowly take our eyes off the rearview mirror and dare to fly right into tomorrow with anticipation, expectation, hope, and a life of open doors.

There are some saving elements about tomorrow, but they are realized only when people like us, with the taste of bread and wine fresh upon our lips, can gather the courage to strike out again, remembering the new covenant of love, humility, purity of heart and meekness. Perhaps then we will enter tomorrow with the feeling of fullness that comes from our first supper. Let this meal symbolize, not the progression away from the things of our pasts that we cling to, but the unknown potentials that life holds for us tomorrow. Let this meal signify an openness to new things. Let this meal symbolize our renewed dedication to the God that gives us this gift of life and, in return, let us assume the responsibilities of serving his greater purposes, his new covenant. Share now your first supper of the new covenant and accept the freedom from the bonds of your pasts that is offered. Know that you are forgiven; accept your acceptance and, in the grace of God and the spirit of the deeper rhythms of life, come now and join the new.

The Drum Major

By Ken Wackes

If one is content to be today
  what he was
    yesterday
He's less today
  than he was
    yesterday
He's dead!
      Hold it, man!
        I don't get it.
          Run that by me again.
If one is content to be today
  what he was
    yesterday
He's less today
  than he was
    yesterday
He's dead!
      Hmmm. If a guy's living
      in the past
        he's dead.

                        Dead?

Kenneth Wackes is a Presbyterian minister teaching in Pompano Beach, Florida.

Hmmm.
To be alive means
   to be open
      to the God who lives—
         who's moving
To be alive means
   to trust
      his proven reliability—
         proven in the way
      the "unknowns" of yesterday
         somehow worked out to be
      the "known" of today
To be alive means
   to await with anticipation the
      fresh
         new
            surprising
   adventure of faith
      of tomorrow
         If a guy's living in
            the past
               he's *dead*.

                                                            Yeh!

To be alive means
   to follow the God of
   Abraham
      Isaac
         Jacob
      I'm getting it now!
         Abraham. . . . . .
            He just packed up and left.

No job waiting for him.
I'll bet
he didn't even
speak the language or
know a soul
in that new place.
Isaac. . . . . .
He hung in there.
Imagine!
Lying on that pile
of rocks. . . .
Your father's knife
ready to do you in!
And Jacob. . . . .
Yeh! I'm getting it now!
Those guys acted
just like a bunch of
. . . . . FOOLS!
To be alive means
to follow the God who is
. . . excitingly alive!
. . . . . "out-in-front"!
the God who leads today in the
"out-in-front" of yesterday
the God who calls today
to anticipate the
"out-in-front" of tomorrow
God's pull on our lives, then, is
from out-ahead
and not from behind
for he is God of the resurrection

and not simply
the grave
I marched in a parade once.
That drum major stole
the show!
Out there in front
of the band.
That's God.
He's out there in front.
When we get there
He's already been there!
Just like
Abraham
Isaac
Jacob
Yeh! The Drum Major!
If God is dead
We are the ones who have
buried him
with our
nostalgia
for the "back-theres"
of yesterday
indolence
in the new things
of today
resistance
to the surprises
of tomorrow
Right on!
And if he's behind us

"back there" someplace
It's because we've taken
        . . . THE WRONG ROAD!
If a guy's living
    in the past
        he's DEAD!
But then the question comes . . . . . .
    Has the "God Who Was"
        ever really existed?
    Isn't his name YAHWEH. . . . I AM
        the God of the living
        and not the dead?
"Come out here, and I will show you
        something NEW!"
        is his promise
            "And I'll never let you down—
            but I'm out *here*
                . . . . . in front!"
Celebrate with me the death of
    the false god of
        meaningless repetition
        nostalgia
        never-challenged-tradition
    the god so easily anticipated
        and out-guessed
    the christ who comes with his
        Protestant Phylacteries
            his membership in the
                Society of Conformity
    the religious Mr. Sand-Man
        Good riddance!

Hurrah!
We're FREE!

FREE! . . . . . .
to not be content to be today
what I was yesterday
to trust my destiny to the hand
of the Lord of the
fresh
surprising
"out-there"
Hold it!
Wait for me!
Let's do it together!
FREE! . . . .
to not be content to be today
what we were yesterday
FREE! . . . .
to trust our lives to the hand
of the Lord of the
fresh
surprising
"out-there"
HE HAS SET US FREE . . . .
TO LIVE!
YESTERDAY!
TODAY!
TOMORROW!

You Make Me Believe in God

By Deryl Fleming

Ruth said, "Entreat me not to leave you or to return from following you; for where you go I will go, and where you lodge I will lodge; your people shall be my people, and your God my God; where you die I will die, and there will I be buried."

—Ruth 1:16-17a

The sermon title is not a dare. It's an affirmation.

First, a story. One word about the significance of what happens. In the days of our story one's geography determined his God. If you lived in Moab you worshiped one god. If you were a Jew you worshiped another. To change one's location usually meant changing one's god. Now the story.

In Bethlehem of Judah the family of Elimelech lived until a famine came. Then they migrated to Moab. There they settled and started over. It was a strange world for them. The two sons married Moabite women who worshiped Chemosh, the god of the Moabites. The years were not easy. During the 10 years they were there both Elimelech and the two sons died. Having heard that the famine in Judah was over, Naomi de-

Deryl Fleming is pastor of Lake Shore Baptist Church, Waco, Texas.

63

cided to return to her homeland and to her own people. She suggested that Ruth and Orpah, the widowed daughters–in–law, remain in Moab with their people. They had offered to go with her to Judah, but she insisted that they stay. They had their own lives to live and Naomi encouraged them to remarry and begin again. Knowing that she could promise them nothing in Judah, she felt that they should stay in Moab. Orpah consented and stayed. But Ruth could not. Naomi said, "See, your sister-in-law has gone back to her people and to her gods; return after your sister-in-law." But Ruth replied, "Entreat me not to leave you or to return from following you; for where you go I will go, and where you lodge I will lodge; your people shall be my people, and your God my God. . . ."

Why Ruth chose to leave all that she had known to go with Naomi is no hard-to-figure-out mystery. It's not difficult to understand why Ruth chose Naomi's God. It was her affection for Naomi. Her deep running friendship—her love for Naomi—was sufficient reason for Ruth to leave the secure womb of the homeland to go out into a future that promised nothing but insecurity. It was reason enough for her to have faith in Naomi's God.

At the risk of sounding trite and sentimental, I want to cast a vote for friendship. In a world so full of both tragedy and joy, friendship is a gift one cannot afford to be without. Someone to weep with and someone to laugh with all of us need. Friendship has a way of adding joy to our joy and diminishing our grief. If one should gain the whole world and have no friends, all would be lost. Friendship is one of God's choicest gifts.

We'll get by with a little help from our friends and with the help of God, which so often comes through those who befriend us. Without the help of friends we would never make it. Nor would we know God's love.

In the effort to encourage his disciples Jesus spoke of their need to love one another, reminding them that a true friend lays his life down for his brother. Further, he reminded them that he was related to them not as master to servant, but friend to friend. "I have called you friends. . . This I command you, to love one another." Knowing the future would bring discouraging and doubtful times, Jesus stressed the importance of their supporting each other. They would better know God's love if they were sure of each other's love.

We don't choose a faith in an isolated, objective study. We grow a faith in the context of life and relationships. That emotion and affection enter into our decisions about God is not bad. It's the way we're made. Pure reason does not exist. We are emotional as well as rational. Our religious preferences are heavily influenced by our history and by those around us. Of that we need not be ashamed, only aware.

For most of us, religion begins with believing in the God of someone else, someone whom we admire and love. A child sees God in the face of his parents, a teenager in the example of another, an adult in the life of a friend.

The shape and color of life and our understanding of God are largely determined by those around us who are "significant others." We are shaped by those who love us. We find faith through those who believe in us and in whom we can believe.

Naomi so lived that Ruth found it possible to accept Naomi's God. You live with faith in God and in me and extend yourself in love to me and I will confess, you make me believe in God.

While grateful for the "peace" on the world scene, we're still uneasy. For one thing, we're not sure it will last. I think one reason for our uneasiness about the truce in Viet Nam is our uneasiness about human relationships. No matter what is accomplished in international relationships, we are still left with the challenge of interpersonal relationships. Not being fully at peace with others, we find it difficult to believe in world peace. Likewise, when we're not at peace with others, we find it impossible to be at peace with God. Not finding people to believe in and who believe in you makes it hard to believe in God and to believe that he believes in you.

I don't know how it began and developed between Ruth and Naomi. Surely it included common human kindness, which may well be the surest witness to divine love. And it may not be all that common. It may be uncommon enough to be convincing. Some of you saw the cartoon we had on the bulletin board picturing a hippie type standing by the roadside. Appearing to be a hitchhiker, he held up a sign to oncoming cars: "I don't want a ride—I just want to say: Have a nice day." Even a kind word can startle you in the midst of a hectic harried day. "Hey, have a good day" is not yet common enough to be trite.

Sharing yourself with another still communicates the most important message of all. Sharing your time, your energy, your being, speaks to the other of his worth to you. And if he's worth that to you, then he's worth something to life. And if to life, then to God.

When you take the time to look at Jesus in the Gospels, you see why he aroused such health and hope in many of those who met him. In going to Zacchaeus' home for dinner Jesus dared to associate with one who was publicly hated. Written off by the Jews as a traitor and a cheat, Zacchaeus was accepted by Jesus as a person of worth. No wonder Zacchaeus and his family were converted. Look at the woman at the well. That he cared enough to stop and talk to her and not condemn her for her continual failure in marriage and life was enough to change her whole being. She went immediately to town to share what had been given her.

Simply put, love is giving yourself to the other. And its power to change, to convince, to motivate, is beyond description. One mark of true love is respect for the other. This doesn't mean that one pays no attention to his own needs. It means that the needs of the other are important too. That his needs are not to be subordinate to mine.

Out of her concern for them Naomi encouraged Orpah and Ruth to stay in Moab. It was not that she didn't want them with her. It was that she wanted them to be free to do what they needed to do. So she encouraged them to stay in their homeland, to remarry and begin again. Orhah did, but Ruth chose not to. The writer tells us that "when Naomi saw that

she was determined to go with her, she said no more."
With Naomi it was okay if Ruth stayed or if she went
with Naomi. She was able to let Ruth decide for herself.

Love is like that. It reaches out to the other, but it
doesn't manipulate or smother. It is always available,
but never pushy. It accepts the other gladly, but does
not force him. It reaches out with gifts and with the
gift of oneself.

Fritz Perls said it like this, "I am not in this world
to live up to your expectations. And you are not in this
world to live up to mine. You are you and I am I. And
if by chance we find each other it's beautiful."

Separateness goes along with authentic together-
ness. By letting the other be who he is, I am free to be
who I am and he is free to become who he can become.
Brainwashing and browbeating may produce a certain
kind of behavior. It doesn't lead to the growth and
development of the person. To silence a person with
your persuasive arguments or show of force or whatever is not to convert him. Love, Paul said, is "the more
excellent way."

The Bible pictures God as going to any extent to hold
out for our freedom to choose. He will not coerce us,
even to receive his love or to give him ours.

The basic thrust of the story is the inclusion of a
foreigner. Ruth's foreignness is carefully underscored.
Her acceptance by Naomi is more like God than like
many of his representatives. Such inclusion is indicative
of a universal love that was not all that common in the
Old Testament world. No matter when the book was
written, its witness to God's universal love is striking.

The Jewish people didn't find it any easier than we do to extend God's love to all. The Old Testament reflects a lot of separatism and snobbishness. In fact, when Jesus appears 300 years after the last of the Old Testament writings, one of his toughest challenges is separatism and exclusiveness. The separatists charge him with associating with the wrong crowd, and they want to keep God's love for themselves.

In our world and Ruth's, to be received by one who might have treated you as a foreigner is to experience God's kind of love. Simon Peter grew up in a segregationist, separatist world, and extending God's love to the Gentile outsiders didn't come naturally. But it came. God spoke to him in a dream, and Peter's mind was changed. He confessed, "Truly I perceive that God shows no partiality, but in every nation anyone who fears him and does what is right is acceptable to him." (Acts 10:34-35)

The Book of Ruth stands as an early witness to the universal love of God that was to be fully revealed in Jesus Christ. That a Moabite woman was chosen to be the great grandmother of David the king reveals that God's hand holds the whole world, not just a corner of it, that he works through all the peoples of the earth to redeem man.

All of us are potential foreigners, and most of us have experienced being an outsider. Yet we pattern our lives so that we're not often reminded of it. We travel in circles where what we do and think is similar to those around us. We forget that our kind of people is not the only kind. The issue is that we cannot afford to forget that all kinds are God's kind.

To be taken in by one who is different, one you might expect to treat you as an outsider, is a humbling and wondrous experience. Nothing is more convincing of the divine love than a human love that reaches across all barriers to include you.

The way others see God is influenced by the way we relate to them, the way we see them and they see us. If they discover in us kindness, respect, and an inclusive spirit they are more likely to find it possible to believe in God as kind, respecting, and inclusive toward them.

It may sound as if I'm laying a heavy burden on you. It is a load of responsibility, but it's not impossible.

To reflect God to others does not mean that we have to be almighty. On the contrary. The person who always seems to be in control is not likely to be of much comfort or encouragement to us. He may get our admiration and respect, but we will not be able to identify with him. Even God went to great pain to suffer with us. Remember that word of Paul to the Corinthian church about the foolishness of the cross and the weakness of God. He reminded them that "the foolishness of God is wiser than men, and the weakness of God is stronger than men." (1 Corinthians 1:25) The Word of God in Christ is not God-above-it, but "God with us." In that realization is a power and wisdom unlike the ordinary and sufficient for hope and courage.

Naomi had not been above it all. She had lost her husband too. And she had not taken it in stride, as though nothing had happened. She felt the bitterness that grief brings. On returning to Bethlehem she told her story. "Do not call me Naomi, call me Mara (which means bitter), for the Almighty has dealt very bitterly with me. I went away full, and the Lord has brought me back empty."

The words Jesus spoke to his disciples about the meaning of his friendship and theirs are set in the context of the last supper, the eve of his betrayal and crucifixion. Not from the stance of one who is exempt from trouble, but from one who is a participant in life's agony, come the words of hope to the disciples. Jesus, too, cried "My God, why have you forsaken me?" He went on to affirm, "Into your hands I commit my life."

To give to another reason to believe in God does not call us to be beyond tragedy and grief, to be an untroubled center of virtue, power, and positive thinking. It requires only that we keep on struggling and striving, and that we care. In fact, it is as a fellow pilgrim that one is best able to help another keep faith. And the strangest thing—in the process of helping another find and keep faith, we are enabled to keep faith. Indeed, *we make each other believe in God.*

Christmas, Rose Gardens, and the Nitty Gritty

By Elliott Massey

Luke 1:26-55 (J. B. Phillips Translation)

Then, six months after Zacharias' vision, the angel Gabriel was sent from God to a Galilean town, Nazareth by name, to a young woman who was engaged to a man called Joseph (a descendant of David). The girl's name was Mary. The angel entered her room and said.

"Greetings to you, Mary. O favored one!—the Lord be with you!"

Mary was deeply perturbed at these words and wondered what such a greeting could possibly mean. But the angel said to her:

"Do not be afraid, Mary; God loves you dearly. You are going to be the mother of a son, and you will call him Jesus. He will be great and will be known as the Son of the most high. The Lord God will give him the throne of his forefather, David, and he will be king over the people of Jacob for ever. His reign shall never end."

One of the great issues of the Christmas event is almost lost in the excitement of the scene at Bethlehem.

Elliott Massey is pastor of Eastwood Christian Church, Nashville, Tennessee.

73

We sometimes forget that the angels had made several visits to earth prior to that holy night. Preparation had to be made for the arrival of the Son of God. And to take care of these matters the angels appeared to Zacharias, who was to be John the Baptist's father, to tell him that his wife, Elizabeth, would have a child. Later the angels visited Joseph to tell him about what was to happen to Mary. The angel Gabriel himself visited Mary and told her of the things that were going to happen and of the birth of Jesus. Mary burst into a magnificent song of praise to the Lord! Think of it— to be told by the chief angel that you are personally ''favored'' and ''loved dearly'' by God! It would be enough to cause anybody to be seized by ecstasy.

But what did this mean?

Well, let's see what it meant for Mary. Almost immediately her world started falling to pieces. Old Simeon in the temple told her that her soul would be pierced with a sword. King Herod ordered that every male child in Bethlehem two years and under be slain, hoping that one of them would be Jesus. And the angel warned Mary of it and this woman, ''favored and loved of God'' as she was, had to get up in the middle of the night and flee to Egypt as a common refugee. There she stayed until Old Herod was dead and the danger past.

But that was only the beginning. As Jesus grew older, he became more difficult to understand. The communication gap widened as he began to gather followers. Many of them wanted to make him king but he wouldn't allow it, and they despised him for that. Others sought revolution and urged him to over-throw the Romans, and he would not. His family thought he was crazy. Others said he was a drunkard and others that he was of the devil.

The religious leaders suspected him as he antago-nized them. The hostility grew. There was public ridi-cule, embarrassment and fear for Mary as she saw her son getting deeper and deeper into trouble. And finally, there was the arrest, the mockery, the trial, and the scourging. And very early one Friday morning this "favored and loved" of God mother stood on a harsh hill and saw her beloved son hanged as a public enemy.

You may be wondering why I talk about these grim things so soon after Christmas. A holiday season is upon us and even now we are preparing for a new year that we hope will be bright and exciting.

I am not morose. I just want to help us keep every-thing in proper perspective. The truth is that the coming of Christ does not put an end to the human scene. For during this very Christmas when houses are full of lighted trees and toys, the hospitals are full of the sick, ambulances wail day and night, autos pile up in carnage, babies die in their cribs, funeral homes are crowded and new graves are opened. The favor and love of God does not exempt us from living out these lives of ours. We have to live in a real world of danger, peril and hurt. No one is excused from that require-ment, not even Mary, the mother of our Lord himself.

Whatever Gabriel meant—whatever the "favor and love" meant—it did not mean a life of ease and comfort. Mary had no fringe benefits. There were no special passes, no reserved seats—no motorcades—no VIP treatment. No dignified escorts to whisk her through the traffic jams of the ordinary life. She had to stop at the traffic lights just like everybody else. There were no secret service agents to shield her from agony, no special residence, no household servants to cater to her whims and no imported chefs to prepare her meals. God never promised her a rose garden and she never got one.

I guess that just here is how we most often approach life. Most of us want a rose garden. And we will do anything, go anywhere, believe anything, trust anybody, that seems promising in acquiring it for us. We hear that Jesus loves us, that God favors us, and that he is able to do for us more than we can ask or imagine. We learn that he works everything out for our good. All we have to do is to love him a little and God goes to work for us . . . so we give him a try. We approach him the same way a selfish nephew would an old, soft hearted, rich aunt. He plays her up, winning and sweet of personality, to win her affection, hoping that she will leave him her house, silverware, and half a million dollars when she kicks off. Such a nephew cares nothing for the old girl herself—but what he can get out of her—and all his sickening fuss over her is but his crafty way of "putting the touch on her."

Well, you don't finagle rose gardens out of God like that! You can't cajole him. And he will not have your affection and praise if he has to buy it from you.

I knew a woman who saw a lovely coat she wanted to buy for her teenage stepson. "Beautiful," I said. "He will love you for it." "Then," she said, "I'll not get it for him. I want Mike to love *me*—not what he thinks I'd do for him *if* he loves me."

Nor can you intimidate or threaten God with ultimatums.

Helen played the piano at church. Her mother took desperately ill and Helen asked God to make her well. No! Helen demanded. She reminded him of the 20 years she had played the piano and told him that if her mother did not recover, she would never play it again. The mother died and Helen kept her word.

What I am saying is that his favor and love are not going to get you a rose garden. And if you are going to church, professing faith in Christ, tithing and praying with that in mind you are headed for disappointment. He is not here to get the monkey off your back. The favor and love of God is not a kind of talisman to ward off the demon that haunts you. It is not meant to deliver you from "the ghosties and the ghoulies and the things that go bump in the night." You cannot carry it in your pocket like a rabbit's foot. It is not a rabbit's foot. It is not magic. It is not a good luck charm. It has no power whatsoever to protect you from the nitty gritty of life.

You ask then, what good is it? Why have his favor at all if he is not going to give me my rose garden? Must his favor and love pierce my soul, too, as it did Mary's?

Well, I have said that God's love does not protect us from the nitty gritty. I believe that is true. And I think it is true just because it is *in* the nitty gritty that God deals with us. He doesn't take us out of it—he redeems us *in* it. This is where we live. The world is not a rose garden. Never was. Never will be. Mary wasn't in one and Jesus was not born in one. But right there, *in* the evil, suffering, sorrowing world, God chose to perform a miracle. Not magic, but a miracle! And he chose Mary, Joseph, Zacharias, and Elizabeth to be part of it. That was what the favor of God did for them. He chose to fulfill his purpose of bringing a touch of the divine into a world full of nitty gritty! Jesus lived with that kind of people—for that's the only kind there are.

When God chooses us it is for the mission that the rest of us shall be blessed by it. We are not singled out for special favors and special blessings for our own consumption. That would be only to swell our own heads and make us insufferable egotists. We are given special blessings because there are duties to perform, burdens to share, hearts to lift and darkness to dispel. And the only thing in life that is worth mentioning is that assurance that somehow the mission of God is being done in us. Every heartache, every cross, every sorrow is bearable if I can be sure of that. For to know that God has chosen me to be an agent of blessing in this world is the surest evidence of favor and love. There is no other—nor is any other needed.

Whatever may be my lot to bear—however grievous my way, however deeply the sword pierces, I know that it is always part of his redemption at work. This was what kept Mary sane at the scene of insanity there at the cross. It was what kept Jesus in his most awesome hours—God was lavishing His favor and love upon him. He was doing a mighty deed, through him.

God does not deal in trifles. He sent a son into the world to redeem men—not to pamper them. Christmas was just the beginning of a drama that would end up in violence, bloodshed, and death. The whole cup of sorrow had to be drained to the dregs. But out of it came the greatest boon to humanity since the world began.

Oh, it is always a dangerous thing to get tangled up with God. Instead of being released, you are invited to danger and dying. And as harsh as that may be, it is, nevertheless, just the way all good comes to the world. Jesus said to his disciples, "Come along and die with me!"

I don't know why it is that way, but I know that it is. People favored of God usually turn out to be people of self-denial, of discipline, and found among those that are hurt and bruised in the earth. God doesn't have any good-time-Charlies! People in rose gardens don't provide much salt for the earth or light or yeast. You see? It is wicked of us to plead for a rose garden when the unfortunate go naked and hungry. Shall we stand before the mirror and admire our own beauty when half of the world is ugly and scarred? Shall we delight in how safe we are when whole cities disappear in fire and earthquake? Shall we rejoice in wholeness and health when there's a man outside the gate full of bloody sores with only a dog for a companion? Shall God be pleased with our prayers of thanksgiving as long as there is **one** of his perishing somewhere? I doubt it. For if you have any favor and love of God at all, it is that you take that with you out there into the nitty gritty world and redeem it.

But take it. And don't be dismayed. God is at work in you! If you feel the sword piercing, don't accuse. Rejoice. Be there—for all those you can serve. For each of them is God's loved one, too. If they were not—if he didn't care about the hungry, the naked, the sick and imprisoned, he would never have asked you to go to them. But he has asked—and that is the very proof that His love and favor are upon *them!* The favor and love of God upon you is his favor and love missioned for the whole world. Through you it is to flourish and prosper so that those now beaten and crushed by the nitty gritty can look up and live again.

One of the good ladies of our own church has brought to mind clearly just what this all means. For many months she sat by the side of her dying husband, ministering to him every way love and devotion can devise. She no more than left the graveside till she was called to leave her home and go be with her brother who was dying of the very same illness that took her husband. And she stayed with him till it was all over. When she returned, I hurried to comfort her, thinking she would be distraught and disconsolate. I expressed my concern and sympathy, which she graciously acknowledged. But I did not find a woman attacking God or saying how unfair life was to bring so much sadness upon her. Rather, I saw a woman with a soft radiance on her countenance and with quiet gratitude in her voice. "Pastor," she said, "God has been so good to me. When my husband and brother needed someone the most, he made it possible for me to be there with them." She had learned what Christmas is really all about—God with us, in the nitty gritty. May we learn it, too!

In the Belly of the Whale: When Hate Should Die

By Harold C. Warlick, Jr.

Many characters in the Bible prove identifiable in our 20th century world. As we sit here today on the downhill side of winter and contemplate the meaning of a cease-fire in our country's longest war, one biblical character especially leaps out at us: the prophet Jonah. Most of us associate Jonah with being swallowed by a legendary whale or giant fish. The book of Jonah, however, is actually a poignant parable about the relation of Israel to other nations. The book skillfully and forcefully calls Israel back to her universal mission of preaching the wideness and totality of God's mercy and forgiveness to *all* nations.

In Jonah's day the Ninevites were enemies of the Jewish people. One day God called Jonah to rise and go to Nineveh for the purpose of preaching to them so they could be saved. Full of disillusionment and hatred, Jonah ran in the opposite direction. According to the legend, he told God that the people of Nineveh were

---

Harold Warlick is pastor of Trinity Baptist Church, Seneca, South Carolina.

not worth saving. Attempting to flee God by ship, Jonah was thrown overboard and engulfed by a giant fish. He resided in the belly of the fish for three days and three nights. In his utter distress he prayed to God constantly but God did not seem to hear him. Finally Jonah was delivered from the belly of the fish. Immediately he journeyed to Nineveh to preach repentance. Alas! the Ninevites repented and God chose to save them. This angered Jonah. He felt that God was turning soft. Embracing his past hatred, he cried out punishment for the "wicked" people.

The crux of the book of Jonah is to be found in the fact that Jonah emerged from the belly of the whale with the same hatreds and limited perceptions which had accompanied him when he began the confinement. In short, he failed to emerge from a trying situation as a new person.

Our nation has been in the belly of the Vietnam war for ten years. Inside this war whale we have prayed to God in distress. Most of the time it has appeared that God has not heard us. Finally, after ten years, not three days, we have been delivered. Now comes the opportunity to preach unity, forgiveness, repentance, and peace.

The crucial question for us as individuals and as a nation is this: what lessons have we learned in the belly of the whale?

Never have we been so clearly called upon to respond to the biblical saying that "I have set before you life and death . . . therefore choose life."

Jonah saw his world with its tragic human problems and traditional boundaries. On the other hand, he heard the voice of God exhorting mercy and kindness for all people. Jonah chose his own convictions as the guideline for behavior, even to the point of voicing anger at God's apparent leniency. We too are cognizant of the tragic human problems in our world. Some of us have lost loved ones trying to deal with these complex and fatal problems. On the other hand, we visualize the Christ and what he stands for—brotherhood, righteousness, and peace. Constantly these two positions are juxtaposed before our eyes. The decision is ours alone. Will we choose life or death? The peace treaty recently signed is only the peak of the iceberg; the rest lies below the surface.

As Christians we must respond to what lies below the surface. We are called to emerge from the belly of the whale a new people. Many of the hard-won gains of civilization are lost in war times: crime rates go up; juvenile delinquency increases; moral retrogression sets in. As Christians we are called to aid the restoration of our society by shifting war-time thoughts and responses to peace-time attitudes and actions. Along with celebrating the return of POWs and MIAs, we must seek repentance and compassion, for this has been an unusual war in several respects. It was the first war in which *civilian* casualties outnumbered military casualties. As we celebrate, then, let us pray that superpowers will take steel out of the land of thatched huts, tanks out of the land of water buffalos and bicycles, and napalm out of the land which barely knows how to use matches. Let us rejoice for this.

Secondly, this was the first war to be fought on television. Even our youngest children had front-row seats for the human suffering. Relay satellites beamed clear pictures to our newspapers the same day that atrocities were taking place.

We cannot pretend that these things have not affected us. Emerging from the belly of the whale after ten years and becoming people of peace will be a difficult task.

Fortunately, Christianity is a religion which deals with the sordid aspects of life. Christianity is something to be done. It is a task to be completed, a way of living life on earth. Christianity makes the absurd claim that individuals can live as peaceful men in a hate-filled world. It is a peaceful religion. Adolf Hitler, according to his chief architect, Albert Speer, often lamented that Germany had the wrong religion. Christianity's not being a religion of the sword diametrically opposed the Nazi dictator's purposes.

Christianity makes the all-encompassing claim that life on earth has a religious purpose. This planet of ours races through the universe at a fantastic rate of speed. It is a transient planet in an exploding universe. Many people take this to mean that life is utterly meaningless, coming from nowhere and going nowhere. They suggest that there is no purpose behind anything that happens in life. They embody Macbeth's haunting description: "full of sound and fury signifying nothing."

The true Christian reasons quite differently. He affirms an ultimate purpose in human life. He contends that even Vietnam is pregnant with positive potentialities. The Christian believes in the theme of the beautiful legend of angels audibly singing over Bethlehem. No one can claim to be Christian who does not enter into that spirit:

> Glory to God on high;
> And on earth peace,
> Good will among men.

Many will argue that this spirit is impractical. Some will say unmitigated optimism such as this cannot function in a world of superpowers, atomic bombs, and napalm. These people argue that the vision of the mountian of the Lord in the Old Testament is a hallucination of the weak and timid. They predict that nations will never beat their swords into plowshares and their spears into pruning forks.

I do know this to be undeniably true: the deaths of men in this war are on our hands. We, the living, will determine whether they died for peace and a new hope—or for nothing.

Consequently we have something very hard to do in the days ahead. We are called to go on a search-and-destroy mission in our own lives. The last mission in any war is assigned to the Christians. We must search out and destroy the last vestige of war. We must pacify our own hearts and minds and conquer the hate and fear that have driven us these past ten years. We have to do this so that 25-30 years from now when men go down life's road without an arm or a leg and small children ask us why, we can respond "Vietnam" and not mean a filthy, obscene memory but instead mean the place where America turned, made a crucial decision, chose life, and climbed out of the belly of the whale a new people.

Seagulls and Saviors

By John Killinger

"He spoke of very simple things—that it is right for a
gull to fly, that freedom is the very nature of his being,
that whatever stands against that freedom must be set
aside, be it ritual or superstition or limitation in any form."
—*Jonathan Livingston Seagull*

"I have come that men may have life, and may have
it in all its fullness."

—John 10:10

One of the images that have caught the imaginations of thousands of persons in recent months is that
of Jonathan Livingston Seagull, the extraordinary
feathered hero of Richard Bach's bestselling novel.

Jonathan's story is simple. He is different from other
gulls—different even from his own parents. He does
not live to eat, as they do, but to fly. The dream of
perfecting his flight, of learning to hurtle through the
skies at ten times the speed of most birds, and then,
stalling, to pull out of awkward and complicated dives
as gracefully as if they were the most natural things

John Killinger is Professor of Preaching and Literature at
Vanderbilt Divinity School, Nashville, Tennessee.

in the world, haunts him day and night. But when he does finally achieve spectacular feats of aerodynamics, the Flock—or "Brotherhood," as it calls itself—shuts him out. Deserted, he continues to work at his flying, mastering greater and greater techniques.

Then one day two unusually white gulls appear to him, one flying at either wing, and conduct him to the heaven of gulls. He is delighted to discover that heaven is not a place of torpor and quiescence, as he had always heard it was, but a wholly new state of learning and achievement. He finds gulls there that have been studying flying much longer than he and can teach him tricks he has never before dreamed of doing. At last, under the tutelage of a very old gull named Chiang, he learns the ultimate trick—how to fly through time and space as if they were not there at all. Chiang, no longer needed, turns brighter and brighter until he disappears. Out of the brightness where none of the gulls can look he speaks his last words. "Jonathan," he says, "keep working on love."

Keep working on love. Jonathan meditates on the words. He finds that he can't stop thinking about the gulls back on Earth. Returning to Earth, he gathers a small group of disciples and begins to instruct them in the rudiments of perfect flying. Rumors spread that he is the Son of the Great Gull. The other gulls puzzle over his simple teachings—"that it is right for a gull to fly, that freedom is the very nature of the gull's being, that whatever stands against that freedom must be set aside, be it ritual or superstition or limitation in any form."

Once, when one of his best students flies head-on into a cliff and lies dead in a flock of screeching, cawing birds, Jonathan talks to him about how control is simply a way of overcoming flight limitations, then touches his wingtip, and the smashed bird flies away. The crowd of gulls, which has become scornful of his difficult teachings, screams that he is a demon. Instantly Jonathan and his pupil transport themselves half a mile away. Why is it, asks Jonathan, that the hardest thing in the world is to convince a gull that he's free? The student doesn't know how Jonathan can love a mob of birds that has just wanted to kill him. You have to look for the good in them, says Jonathan. "You have to practice and see the real gull, the good in every one of them, and to help them see it in themselves."

Jonathan sends his pupil back to the flock to work with the outcasts, and he himself, shimmering in the air until he becomes transparent, flies away to instruct other birds in other flocks. Before he goes, however, he warns the student not to let them spread silly rumors about him, or make him a god. "I'm a seagull," he says. "I like to fly."

What Bach has done, of course, is to take the stories of several persons—Socrates, Buddha, Confucius, Chuang Tzu, Jesus, Mohammed, perhaps even Martin Luther King and Gloria Steinem—and weave them into a modern allegory where each reader can interpret the meaning almost any way he wishes. One thing is certain, however: the story is not about birds—it is about people.

The Christian will undoubtedly recognize in the saga

of Jonathan Seagull many bits and pieces of the image of Jesus—his dream of perfected humanity, his apparently miraculous deeds, his way of caring for even those persons who ultimately rejected him, and his constant concern that his disciples themselves become embodiments of love.

If we interpret the story this way, we also open ourselves to the novelist's warning about Jesusolatry. "Don't let them spread silly rumors," said Jonathan, "or make me into a god. I'm just a seagull who likes to fly."

It is easier to make Jesus into a god. It removes the necessity for us to do his works after him. After all, we reason, if he is a god how can we hope to imitate him with real success? So we are out from under, so to speak; we let him be the god and assume all the responsibility.

Bach may be a better theologian than many orthodox Christians on this point. At least, many biblical experts have been trying for some time now to tell us that the divinization of Jesus was not something Jesus asked for but something the church came to insist on after his death. It was easier to market a god than it was to market a crucified idealist.

Speaking of the church, I wonder where you would identify it in the seagull story. Is it the little group of disciples which Jonathan trains to take over his work? Or do you see it more obviously in the flock of screeching gabbling birds that live to eat, not to fly, and make outcasts of any birds that really take Jonathan's words seriously?

I'm afraid it has been my experience that we are often more faithfully represented by the latter picture than by the former. We tend so easily to lapse into querulousness and uncharitableness. Losing the master design of the faith, we fall into patterns of pettiness and greed and insecurity like all the rest of the world. We are no more open or free than other parts of society. Religion itself becomes a kind of prison, or a platform of legalism from which we mount assaults on those who threaten us or disagree with us. We use the church as a means of justifying our perceptual limitations and societal disorders.

If this is true, then perhaps the allegory of the gulls helps us to see ourselves better, and to hear the gospel we haven't been hearing very clearly in our customary words and phrases. Man was not made for grubbing a living, it says, but for exploring new possibilities and expanding his boundaries. Humanity needs freedom, and whatever stands in the way of freedom— even if it does so in the name of ritual or religion— must be set aside.

The picture of Jesus himself becomes clearer when we recall how insistent he was on this very point. He came that we might have life, he said. His whole ministry was summed up in the phrase about proclaiming "release to the captives." As one famous biblical scholar said in the title of a recent book, "Jesus *means* freedom."

But releasing captives always means upsetting the economy that has depended on captivity. Slaves cannot be set free without destroying the kingdoms of the slaveholders. And therefore release always entails a battle. Jesus was crucified in such a battle. Somebody always gets hurt in the struggle, because the powers of darkness do not give up easily. There are bound to be crucifixions, assassinations, slanderings, misunderstandings.

Yet Jonathan, like Jesus, speaks of loving the flock, of caring for the masses, even those who are blindly bent on crucifying or destroying the good.

Loving, says Jonathan, is looking for the real gull, the potential gull, that gull that can emerge from the blind and limited gull, and then helping that gull to come into being, to develop out of the old gull. "That's what I mean by love," he says. "It's fun when you get the knack of it."

Maybe there's an insight here into the nature of love that we haven't thought about lately. Love isn't responding positively to what the eye is able to see. At least, if that can be called love, it isn't the best kind of love. It is only conditional love. It says, "I will love you *if* . . .
. . . if you maintain your attractiveness
. . . if you treat me the way I like to be treated
. . . if you conform to the patterns which I find
most desirable for you.
But genuine love isn't conditioned on what is or meets the eye. It responds to what cannot be seen, to what exists only in potentiality or possibility. It sees the flower in the seed and the angel in the stone.

What *should* we be in the church? if we love the way Jesus loved we will look beyond appearances to the potential of every person. We will be a fellowship where persistent caring helps the best to emerge in everyone. We will be a group of people in whom forgiveness is so active and tangible that the ordinary mechanisms of repression and withdrawal are no longer needed, and lives can unfold with naturalness and openness, like blossoms in the sun. We will be the real and actual body of Christ, where therapy goes on so constantly that the resurrection of the dead is known as an experiential reality and not as an incomprehensible test of creedal loyalty.

It might even be fun if we got the knack of it!